The Bir

by Laura Elizabeth
illustrated by Holli Conger

I like to help my dad.
We get up early.
We are very quiet.

We eat breakfast.

I like to ride
in the truck.

We get wood.
We put it in the truck.

My dad gets the
hammer and nails.

My dad hammers the
nails. I help, too.

I like to help my dad.
The birds like it, too.